CHILDREN'S BOOK PRESS • SAN FRANCISCO, CALIFORNIA

The People Shall Continue

Written by Simon Ortiz

Illustrated by Sharol Graves

MANY, many years ago, all things came to be.
The stars, rocks, plants, rivers, animals.
Mountains, sun, moon, birds, all things.
And the People were born.
Some say, "From the ocean."
Some say, "From a hollow log."
Some say, "From an opening in the ground."
Some say, "From the mountains."
And the People came to live
in the Northern Mountains and on the Plains,
in the Western Hills and on the Seacoasts,
in the Southern Deserts and in the Canyons,
in the Eastern Woodlands and on the Piedmonts.

Revised edition © 1988, original edition © 1977 by Children's Book Press. All rights reserved. Printed in Hong Kong through Interprint, San Francisco.
CIP data may be found on page 24.

Some People fished, others were hunters.
Some People farmed, others were artisans.
Their leaders were those who served the People.
Their healers were those who cared for the People.
Their hunters were those who provided for the People.
Their warriors were those who protected the People.
The teachers and the elders of the People
all taught this important knowledge:
  "The Earth is the source of all life.
   She gives birth.
   Her children continue the life of the Earth.
   The People must be responsible to her.
   This is the way that all life continues."

The People of the many Nations visited
each other's lands.
The People from the North brought elk meat.
The People from the West gave them fish.
The People from the South brought corn.
The People from the East gave them hides.
When there were arguments,
their leaders would say,
    "Let us respect each other.
    We will bring you corn and baskets.
    You will bring us meat and flint knives.
    That way we will live a peaceful life.
    We must respect each other, and the animals,
    the plants, the land, the universe.
    We have much to learn from all the Nations."

Nevertheless, life was always hard.
At times, corn did not grow and there was famine.
At times, winters were very cold and there was hardship.
At times, the winds blew hot and rivers dried.
At times, the People grew uneasy among themselves.
The learned men and women talked with each other
about what to do for their People,
but it was always hard.
They had to have great patience
and they told their People,
    "We should not ever take anything for granted.
    In order for our life to continue,
    we must struggle very hard for it."

But one day, something unusual began to happen.

Maybe there was a small change in the wind.
Maybe there was a shift in the stars.
Maybe it was a dream that someone dreamed.
Maybe it was the strange behavior of an animal.
The People thought and remembered,
    "A long time ago, there were Yellow-skinned men
      who came upon the ocean to the Western Coasts."
The People thought and remembered,
    "A long time ago, there were Red-haired men
      who came upon the ocean to the Eastern Coasts."
But these visitors had not stayed for long.
They met with some of the People
and soon they left upon the ocean for their homes.

But now, the People began to hear fearful stories.

Strange men had arrived on the shores of the South.
Spanish, these men called themselves.
They came seeking treasures and slaves.
These men caused destruction among the People.
The Nations of the South were burned
by heedless and forceful men.

9

Soon, there were other dreadful stories.

More men, these with their wives and children,
arrived on the Eastern Coasts.
English, French, Dutch, they called themselves.
They spoke with a fervor that frightened
the People who met with them.
They taught about a God whom all should obey.
They said they were special men of this God.

Soon, the People saw the destruction
of their Nations.
They soon found out it was the aim
of the English, French, and Dutch to take their lands.
The rich and the powerful of these men
formed an American government.
They wanted the land because
it was fertile with forests and farmland
and wealthy with precious minerals.
And they wanted the People to serve them as slaves.

When the People saw these men did not respect them and the land, they said,
   "We must fight to protect ourselves and the land."
In the West, Popé called warriors from the Pueblo and Apache Nations.
In the East, Tecumseh gathered the Shawnee and the Nations of the Great Lakes, the Appalachians, and the Ohio Valley to fight for their People.
In the Midwest, Black Hawk fought to save the Sauk and Fox Nation.
In the Great Plains, Crazy Horse led the Sioux in the struggle to keep their land.
Osceola in the Southeast, Geronimo in the Southwest, Chief Joseph in the Northwest, Sitting Bull, Captain Jack, all were warriors.

They were warriors who resisted and fought
to keep the American colonial power from taking their lands.

From the 1500's to the late years of the 1800's,
the People fought for their lives and lands.
In battle after battle, they fought until they grew weak.
Their food supplies were gone, and their warriors were killed or imprisoned.
And then the People began to settle
for agreements with the American government.

13

The leaders of the People agreed to Treaties.
The People said they would stop their armed fight.
The Americans promised the People
they could live on land they both agreed
was the People's land.
Upon this land, the People could hunt
and fish and have their sacred ceremonies.
Upon this land, the Nations of the People could live.
The People thought,
    "The Earth is the source of all life."
They knew they must have the courage to continue.
The People promised to honor the Treaties.

The People had to agree to live on reservations.
Much of the reservation land was very poor.
There were no more buffalo to hunt
and the deer and elk were scarce.
Many of the People ran away
and they were forced back by the Americans.
The Nations of the People were weakened.
They were broken in united strength.

Soon, more Americans came.
They were gold miners, railroad men,
outlaws, missionaries, ranchers.
They wanted the rest of the land the People had.
Treaties were broken by them
and the reservations grew even smaller.

The Americans sent government agents.
They told the People they could not live
the way they had before.
The missionaries asked the goverment
to put a stop to the sacred ceremonies,
the dances, and the songs of the People.

The government agents gathered the children.
They took the children to boarding schools
far from their homes and families.
The children from the West
were taken to the East.
The children from the East
were taken to the West.
The People's children were scattered
like leaves torn from a tree.
At schools far from home,
the children were taught to become Americans.
They learned to be ashamed of their People.

The People went to schools.
They went to Christian churches.
They served in the American army.
Some even almost became Americans.
But they were still the People.
They farmed and raised livestock.
They made and sold crafts for a living.
Nevertheless, the People were very poor.
There were no jobs on the reservations.
Even though they didn't want to,
many of the People had to leave.

They were moved by the government
into the cities across America.
Oakland, Cleveland, Chicago, Dallas,
Denver, Phoenix, Los Angeles.
They worked in factories, on railroads,
in businesses, even for the government.
Often they were discouraged
and their families suffered in the cities.
They struggled hard for their lives.

All this time, the People remembered.
Parents told their children,
    "You are Shawnee. You are Lakota.
    You are Pima. You are Acoma.
    You are Tlingit. You are Mohawk.
    You are all these Nations of the People."
The People told each other,
    "This is the life of our People.
    These are the stories and these are the songs.
    This is our heritage."
And the children listened.

The parents said,
    "This has been the struggle of our People.
    We have suffered but we have endured."
Listen, they said, and they sang the songs.
Listen, they said, and they told the stories.
Listen, they said, this is the way our People live.

All across America,
the Nations of the People were talking.
The Cheyennes in the cities and the Navajos in the country.
The Seminoles in Los Angeles and the Cherokees in Oklahoma.
The Chippewa in Red Lake and the Sioux in Denver.
Everywhere, the People on the reservations,
in small towns, in the large cities --
they were talking, and they were listening.

They were listening to the words
of the elder People who were speaking.
    "This is the life that includes you.
    This is the land that is yours.
    All these things that were pushed away from us
    and broken by the American powers and government,
    they are alive, and we must keep them alive.
    All these things will help us to continue."

Once again, the People realized
what was happening to the land.
They realized it was the powerful forces
of the rich and the government
that made the People suffer.

The People looked around them
and they saw Black People, Chicano People,
Asian People, many White People and others
who were kept poor by American wealth and power.
The People saw that these People
who were not rich and powerful shared
a common life with them.
The People realized they must share
their history with them.

"We shall tell you of our struggles," they said.
"We are all the People of this land.
 We were created out of the forces
 of earth and sky, the stars and water.
 We must make sure that the balance of the Earth be kept.
 There is no other way.
 We must struggle for our lives.
 We must take great care with each other.
 We must share our concern with each other.
 Nothing is separate from us.
 We are all one body of People.
 We must struggle to share our human lives with each other.
 We must fight against those forces
 which will take our humanity from us.
 We must ensure that life continues.
 We must be responsible to that life.
 With that humanity and the strength
 which comes from our shared responsibility
 for this life, the People shall continue."

The People Shall Continue

This is an epic story of Native American People. It extends in time from the Creation to the present day; it touches all aspects of life; it speaks in the rhythms of traditional oral narrative.

Essentially, this is a teaching story, as are most Native American stories. Its purpose is to instill a sense of responsibility for life. The creation of life was no accident, it says. It was with a deliberate purpose that all things came to be.

The words of the story transmit the spirit of the People, as well as information about what has come before. It makes no difference that the story is told in English rather than in one of the many Native languages. In the hands of a true tribal storyteller, the words make a picture of life as it has actually been and as it continues to be.

In the last part of the story the concept of "the People" is enlarged to include all Peoples now living on this land who have been the victims of inhumanity. The storyteller turns to all of us and says that we must be responsible. "We must take great care with each other," he says.
"We must fight against those forces
which will take our humanity from us.
We must ensure that life continues."

Children's Book Press is especially grateful to J.R. Howard, Wilma Mankiller, Beryl LaRose, and the students and teachers of the Oakland Native American Survival School for their guidance during the early stages of this project.

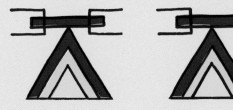

Harriet Rohmer
Series Editor

Book Design: Harriet Rohmer, Robin Cherin, Roger I Reyes
Lettering: Roger I Reyes
Production: Robin Cherin

Library of Congress Cataloging-in-Publication Data

Ortiz, Simon J.
    The people shall continue.

    Summary: Traces the progress of the Indians of North America from the time of the Creation to the present.
    1. Indians of North America—History—Juvenile literature. [1. Indians of North America—History] I. Graves, Sharol, ill. II. Title.
E77.4.O77 1988   970.004'97   88-18929
ISBN 0-89239-041-7

DUE DATE